New Testament

Treasures

Reflections and prayers
on favourite Bible passages

Nick Fawcett

kevin
mayhew

First published in 2004 by

KEVIN MAYHEW LTD

Buxhall, Stowmarket, Suffolk, IP14 3BW

E-mail: info@kevinmayhewltd.com

KINGSGATE PUBLISHING INC

1000 Pannell Street, Suite G, Columbia, MO 65201

E-mail: sales@kingsgatepublishing.com

The material in this book first appeared in *Daily Prayer*
and *The Fawcett Bible Studies*.

9 8 7 6 5 4 3 2 1 0

ISBN 1 84417 263 5

Catalogue No. 1500705

Cover design by Angela Selfe

Edited by Katherine Laidler

Typesetting by Fiona Connell-Finch

Printed and bound in Great Britain

Contents

Introduction

Some passages of the Bible stand out in the memory, don't they? While the whole of Scripture is important, neglected at our peril, certain verses capture our imagination or speak to us in a way that few others can begin to. Who can forget the words of the 23rd Psalm, the parables of Jesus, or the wonderful teaching of Paul in 1 Corinthians 13 on the gift of love? These are just some of the countless passages to have encouraged, comforted, strengthened and inspired Christians across the centuries.

We must, of course, beware of being too selective when it comes to reading the Bible, or we will end up avoiding whatever might challenge our particular viewpoint, thus effectively closing our ears to anything that God might wish to say to us. He has an uncanny knack of speaking through the most unlikely of verses, stretching our horizons and disturbing the comfortable status quo. On the other hand, well-loved verses can remind us of the underlying realities of the gospel, offering reassurance in times of doubt, support in times of challenge and hope in times of despair. Some, indeed, become so familiar to us that they seem almost like old friends. We may even know them off by heart, yet their power to challenge, inspire and encourage remains undiminished, God continuing to speak through them in new and wonderful ways.

In this short compilation I have drawn upon my book *Daily Prayer* and various volumes of my Bible Study series to offer brief reflections on 16 unforgettable passages selected from the New Testament epistles and the book of Revelation, each supplemented by a simple closing prayer. The selection is inevitably a personal one, but I suspect many of the passages I have chosen will also feature among your own personal favourites. It is my hope that they will speak as powerfully to you as they have to me.   NICK FAWCETT

Romans 7:15, 19-25
Why do I do it?

I do not understand why I act as I do. For I keep on doing what I hate rather than the things I yearn to do. Instead of the good that I intend, I do evil. Now if I do what I don't really want to do, it can no longer be me doing it but must be sin dwelling within me. I find it to be a law that whenever I intend to do good, evil is there as well, for, while deep within I delight in the law of God, I see a different law in my body that battles with the law of my mind, holding me captive to the law of sin that dwells in my members. What a miserable creature I am! Who will deliver me from this body of death? Thank God, he will do so through Jesus Christ our Lord!

Reflection

Why did I do it? How often have you asked yourself that question? Just like the Apostle Paul, we frequently find ourselves doing exactly the opposite of what we intend. The reasons, of course, are many and varied: greed, envy, lust and pride, to name but a few. Yet why is it that we struggle sometimes to control such failings, no matter how much we long to? That is a much deeper question, which people will answer in different ways according to their perspective on life. For Paul it pointed to the essentially fallen nature of humanity: what some might term original sin; what others would simply call human weakness. We could debate the issues involved for the rest of our days and still not exhaust them. Similarly, we could struggle to overcome our faults with every fibre of our body, yet be no nearer success at the end than at the beginning.

Thankfully, as Paul reminds us, we can also spend the rest of our days, and those beyond, at peace with God and ourselves, for what *we* cannot achieve *he* has decisively accomplished through his living, dying and rising among us in Christ. In him we are made new, whatever keeps us from God absolved, nailed to the cross as if it had never been. No wonder Paul ended his outburst of frustration in an outpouring of praise: 'Thank God, he will do so through Jesus Christ our Lord!'

Prayer

Merciful Lord,
  assured of your forgiveness
  and with my heart at peace,
  I celebrate your goodness,
  the past put behind me,
  the future full of promise.
Receive my praise,
in the name of Christ.
Amen.

Romans 8:1-2, 38-39
No condemnation

There is, then, no condemnation now for those in Christ Jesus, because the law of the Spirit of life has set us free from the law of sin and death. I am convinced that nothing can separate us from Christ's love. Neither death nor life, nor angels nor demons, nor the present nor the future, nor any powers, nor height nor depth nor anything else in all creation, will ever be able to separate us from the love of God that is ours in Jesus Christ our Lord.

Reflection

Why is it that a piece of string, no matter how carefully you put it away in a drawer, always gets tangled into knots? Even more perplexing, how is it that children's shoelaces, however painstakingly you may tie them, manage to come undone within a few paces? Whoever could answer such mysteries would be a rich person indeed! Doing and undoing: those opposites seem, in fact, to underly so many problems in life. Tackle a pile of washing-up or ironing, mow the lawn or weed the garden, clean the car or paint the house, and before you know it the job needs doing again. But make one simple mistake and, however hard we try, we can't undo it. Or can we?

At the heart of our faith lies a triumphant message of something both done and undone. On the one hand, nothing can undo what God has done in Christ. Through his death and resurrection, he has destroyed the power of evil and opened the way to life for all. What needed doing has been done, and nothing can ever change that!

Yet, on the other hand, through that decisive act, everything else done can be undone, for God is always ready to put the past behind us and to help us start again. To assume that we are bound by what has gone before is to deny the glorious resurrection message. Whatever we are, or have been, we can always be a new creation! The past is done with, the future is open – thanks be to God!

Prayer
Lord Jesus Christ,
>   for the victory you have won over sin and death,
>   and the victories you continue to win in my life,
>   receive my praise.
Amen.

Romans 8:28

All things working together for good

We know that all things work together for good with those who love God, who have been called according to his purpose.

Reflection

It sounds wonderful, doesn't it? – 'all things working together for good with those who love God' – but is it true? The stark realities of life very often seem to say otherwise, for so much seems to deny God's goodness and contradict his love. In what ways, for example, do things work together for good in the life of someone dying from cancer, the victim of a terrorist bomb, the parent of a murdered child, the person maimed in a road accident or the loved one struck down with Alzheimer's? Any simplistic idea that God delivers us from life's sufferings and traumas is kicked firmly into touch by such experiences, the Christian being as vulnerable to them as any. But Paul, of course, does not for a moment intend to suggest otherwise. His faith, remember, was in the God whose Son had been cruelly flogged and then nailed to a cross, condemned to a slow and agonising death. And Paul himself, in the cause of Christ, had endured flogging, stoning, hardship and imprisonment. Discipleship was anything but a bed of roses. The 'good' he had in mind went deeper than any superficial under-standing of the word, being rooted in his conviction of God's love beyond death. Without that faith in his ever-lasting purpose, all talk of his goodness would be rendered void, exposed as an empty illusion. In the empty tomb and risen Christ, however, we are brought face to face with the God who brings light out of darkness, hope out of despair, good out of evil. And for Paul, while that transforming power is only fully realised through resurrection into God's kingdom, it is true in microcosm here and now, God being able to bring something positive out of sorrow and suffering, turmoil and tragedy. That is our faith: not a naïve belief that Christian commitment guarantees exemption from life's tribulations, but an inner assurance that even our darkest hour can yield something of value, speaking of God's love and pointing towards the eternal blessings he holds in store.

Prayer

Gracious God,
    in the good and the bad,
    the happy and the sad,
    help me to keep on trusting you,
    confident that your purpose will win through
    and your love triumph,
    through Jesus Christ my Lord.
Amen.

1 Corinthians 1:26-29
Use for the 'useless'

Consider the nature of your calling. Not many of you were wise in human terms; not many were important; not many were well born. God, however, chose the foolish of this world in order to shame the wise, the weak to shame the strong, the lowest and the despised – those considered as nothing – to quash those who consider themselves something, so that nobody may boast before him.

Reflection

It looked to me like a pile of old junk – a curious assortment of bric-a-brac and cast-offs barely worth a second glance. Clearly, however, some people saw things differently, for there was a queue outside waiting for the doors to open and the mad scramble to begin. I never felt altogether comfortable at those jumble sales, for I was keenly aware that for some people the goods on sale there represented all they could afford, yet in my first church they were a fact of life – the only way to keep the doors open and keep me in a job. I learned something useful, however, from the experience; namely, that what might seem useless to one person can be anything but to another – a lesson that is equally applicable when it comes to assessing the worth of individuals. All too easily we write people off, judging them by our own set of values and concluding that they fail to pass muster.

Strangely, we can do the same of ourselves, convinced that there is no way God can possibly use us. He, however, invariably has other ideas, able to use us in the most unexpected and surprising of ways. Never consider that you or anyone else is useless, for as far as God is concerned, 'useless' is a word that doesn't exist.

Prayer

Living God,
    forgive me for overlooking my own potential
    and closing my mind to that in those around me.
Forgive me for finding it so easy to put people down
    and so hard to build them up.
Teach me to recognise that everyone has a place
    in your purpose
    and a contribution to make to your kingdom,
    and so help me to be open to all you are able to do,
    through others and through me.
In Christ's name I ask it.
Amen.

1 Corinthians 9:24-27
Pressing on

Do you not know that though all may run in a race, only one receives the prize. Run, therefore, so that you may be the one who obtains it. Athletes wrestle to discipline their bodies, so that they may receive an award that ultimately perishes, but we strive for an imperishable award. In consequence, I do not run aimlessly, nor do I box as though I am pummelling thin air, but I subject my body to punishment to make sure that, having announced the race to others, I am not disqualified from it myself.

Reflection

A while back, I challenged a friend to a game of squash. It seemed a good idea at the time – that is, until I started to play! Two truths then swiftly dawned on me. The first was that my opponent was in a different league to me, hardly surprising given that he played the game two or three times a week. The second was that I was a lot less fit than I thought I was. That, too, should have come as no surprise, for it was my first game of squash for 25 years and virtually my first serious exercise in all that time, but, in common with most of us, I fondly liked to imagine that I was still as youthful and energetic as I'd been in my teens. To realise how out of condition I was came as something of a shock and brought home to me the need for some kind of fitness programme to make up for the long hours stuck behind a desk.

There are clear parallels in all this with Christian discipleship. Most of us like to imagine that we are in tiptop spiritual condition, but the reality may be very different.

Though we'd never admit it, our relationship with Christ becomes an occasional pursuit rather than an ongoing commitment. We jog along casually as the mood takes us, rarely stretching the muscles of faith, let alone getting ourselves into the sort of shape needed to run a marathon and see it through to the end. Hopefully we will success-fully complete the course, but there is a very real risk that we may run out of steam along the way. Don't let's be deceived, putting our trust in the efforts and achievements of yesterday. The prize is there before us – are we resolved to make it ours?

Prayer

Living God,
    I talk of commitment,
    yet so often I am casual and complacent in discipleship.
Instead of seeking to grow in faith,
    I assume I have advanced as far as I need to.
Forgive me my feeble vision and lack of dedication.
Instil in me a new sense of purpose
    and a greater resolve to run the race,
    and so help me to achieve the prize
    to which you have called me in Jesus Christ,
    for his name's sake.
Amen.

1 Corinthians 13:4-7

The greatest gift

Love is patient and kind; it is not jealous or puffed up with its own importance, vaunting itself before others, nor does it knowingly cause offence. It does not seek its own well-being, is not easily provoked, and does not think evil or rejoice in wrongdoing, but rejoices rather in the truth. It embraces all things, believes all things, hopes all things, endures all things.

Reflection

Many years ago I was given a copy of a poem, the author of which I have never discovered, on the subject of friendship. It speaks of those 'who will not run away . . . but will stop and stay', even when they see our darker side, the aspects of our character we prefer to keep hidden: 'a friend who, far beyond the feebleness of any vow or tie, will touch the secret place where I am really I'. I like that, for it speaks not only of true friendship but also of love. We bandy the word around so much, don't we? – in church as much as anywhere – yet we rarely get close to understanding what it means. Another poem, this time by William Shakespeare, encapsulates the qualities at its heart: 'Love is not love which alters when it alteration finds . . . O no! it is an ever-fixed mark.'

Yet neither of these two examples can quite match the timeless words of Paul in his letter to the Corinthians. There is enough here to reflect on for a lifetime and still not exhaust it, but, for me, one thing Paul says stands out: the willingness of love to believe the best. We see this exemplified in the ministry of Jesus. Where others saw reason to condemn, he offered forgiveness; where others saw evil, he saw good. He knew the worst of people yet he saw also the best. Isn't that what should mark us out as Christians? We are not called to be naïvely idealistic, pretending people are better than they really are, nor are we expected to ignore their faults and attribute non-existent virtues. What we *are* asked to do, is to see the positive as well as the negative, the potential for good as well as the capacity for evil. Do that, and we will begin to understand what it means to love and why love is so special.

Prayer

Gracious God,
    break through my narrow judgemental attitudes
    and help me to look at the world through your eyes.
As you have seen the good in me,
    so help me to see the good in others,
    the best in all,
    through Jesus Christ my Lord.
Amen.

1 Corinthians 15:20-22, 51-52
Resurrection hope

Now Christ has been raised from the dead, and become
the first fruits for those who have fallen asleep. For, just
as death came through one man, so also the resurrection
of the dead comes through one man. As in Adam all die,
so also in Christ will all be brought back to life. Listen
and I will tell you a mystery. We will not all sleep for
ever, but at the last trumpet we will all be changed, in a
moment, in the twinkling of an eye, for a trumpet will
sound and the dead will be raised to immortal life, and
we shall be changed!

Reflection

During the dark years of the Second World War there
was a song that was to become a firm favourite among
troops and civilians alike, bringing solace, encourage-
ment and inspiration to those separated from friends and
loved ones. That song, of course, sung by the Forces' sweet-
heart Vera Lynn, was 'We'll meet again'. Tragically, many
never did meet again, thousands losing their lives in the
far-flung fields of battle. That conflict, like the one that had
preceded it such a short time before, starkly brought home
the reality of death to innumerable families, few untouched
by the loss of a son, husband, brother or other relation.

Today, by contrast, we can push our mortality under
the carpet; death, as has often been observed, being the
great social taboo of our time. So how should we view it?
Is it something to dread, a step into a terrifying unknown?
Is it a cause for despair, the last enemy that makes a
mockery of all our hopes and striving? It is for many, but

it shouldn't be, for the message of the gospel is that death has been defeated; Christ has won new life for all through the cross and the empty tomb. Naturally, the prospect of dying remains unwelcome, whether it be our own death or that of our loved ones, for it still entails the heartbreak of separation and ensuing sense of isolation for those who are bereaved. Words can never express the pain and inner turmoil that losing someone close to us involves. Yet we believe it is not the end of the story but rather the start of a new chapter; a chapter in which, one day, we'll meet again.

Prayer

Living God,
>teach me to look beyond the apparent finality of death
>to the new life you hold for all your people,
>and help me to rest secure in the assurance
>that death is not the end
>but a new beginning;
>a stepping stone into your glorious kingdom,
>in which death shall be no more
>and where all will rejoice in the wonder of your love,
>for evermore.

Amen.

2 Corinthians 5:17
Lovingly restored

Anyone united with Christ is a new creation; the old self
has passed away in its entirety; everything is made new.

Reflection

It was an act that shocked the nation: an internationally
renowned painting wantonly vandalised by a knife-
wielding madman in a frenzied and motiveless attack.
What once had been a priceless masterpiece was suddenly
a shredded piece of canvas hanging forlornly from its
frame; a pathetic reminder of what should have been.
Could it be saved? Incredibly, yes! Through a long, loving
and painstaking process it was finally restored to something
like its original splendour.

To the eye of faith there are parallels here with the
message of the gospel. Each of us is fashioned by God in
his likeness, unique and precious to him, but weakness
and disobedience so disfigure our lives that they become
a travesty of what he intended. Yet he refuses to give up
on us. However long it takes, he is constantly striving to
restore and remake us, to recreate us in the likeness of
Christ. We cannot achieve this by ourselves, however
hard we try, but thankfully it does not rest finally with us.
The good news of Christ centres around new beginnings,
a fresh start not of our own making but made possible by
the grace of God. Does that mean we are suddenly made
perfect? Not a bit of it – the scars left by the old self are
still sometimes all too obvious – but in God's eyes we
have been restored through Christ. However often you
fail, and however frustrated you may be at your inability

to live the way you want to, never lose sight of the fact that God accepts you as you are and is at work every moment of each day to bring his new creation to perfection.

Prayer

Loving Lord,
    I thank you that you are a God
    who makes all things new;
    that, despite my lack of faith and many faults,
    you never give up on me,
    but patiently strive to recreate me
    through the power of your Holy Spirit.
Come to me now in all my weakness,
    and, by your grace,
    renew,
    redeem
    and restore me in the likeness of Christ,
    for his name's sake.
Amen.

2 Corinthians 12:9-10

Strength in weakness

He has said to me, 'My grace is enough for you, for my power is made perfect in weakness.' Therefore, I will gladly boast of my weaknesses that allow the power of Christ to work within me. I am more than happy to endure weakness, abuse, privation, persecution and misfortune for the sake of Christ; for the weaker I am, the stronger I become.

Reflection

What does it mean to talk about strength in weakness? The idea sounds nonsensical, a contradiction in terms, and, wrongly understood, it is precisely that. If we imagine that every frailty is in fact a source of power, every Achilles' heel the secret of some Herculean endowment, then we are in for a rude surprise. Weakness in itself is nothing to be proud of. What matters is how we deal with it: whether we deny it and struggle on regardless or whether we are honest enough to admit our need and seek help from others. That's what Paul had in mind when writing to the Corinthians. He knew that his own resources were hopelessly inadequate to meet the task to which God had called him – the task of taking the gospel out into the world. But recognising that truth – his utter dependence on divine grace – opened the way to God using him in ways beyond his imagining. Had he relied on his own efforts and ingenuity he could have achieved nothing, but with God working through him, given free reign, all things were possible.

What was true for Paul is true also for us. God, and

God alone, is able to turn weakness into strength. The more we understand that, the more he can work in and through us. Much in daily life, let alone Christian discipleship, may seem beyond us, and were it down to us alone we'd be right in thinking so. But if we acknowledge that fact humbly and sincerely before God, asking him to fill and transform us through his Spirit, we will find his strength made perfect in weakness.

Prayer

Sovereign God,
    faced by the demands and difficulties life presents
    I feel overwhelmed sometimes,
    questioning my ability to get through.
Faced by the countless needs of the world,
    I feel there is nothing I can do,
    no way I can make a difference.
Faced by your call to discipleship,
    your call to love and shed light in the lives of others,
    I feel it is beyond me,
    impossible even to come near.
Help me to understand, though,
    that it is in those very weaknesses
    that your strength is most perfectly seen,
    provided I acknowledge them honestly to you
    and open my life to your renewing power
    and transforming love.
Take me, then, with all my faults and failings,
    and use me as you will,
    through Jesus Christ my Lord.
Amen.

Ephesians 6:11-17
Equipped for battle

Don the whole armour of God, so that you may be able to withstand the ruses of the devil. For we do battle, not with flesh and blood, but with the rulers, authorities and cosmic powers of darkness – with the spiritual forces of evil in high places. So, then, take up God's heavenly armour, so that you may be able to resist on that evil day, standing firm come what may. Stand, therefore, and secure the belt of truth around your waist, and put on the breastplate of righteousness. Shoe your feet with a readiness to proclaim the gospel of peace. Above all, grasp the shield of faith, with which you will be able to smother the flaming arrows of the evil one. Take also, by prayer and supplication, the helmet of salvation, and the sword of the Spirit, which is the word of God.

Reflection
One of the biggest box office hits of recent years was the film *Gladiator*, a movie that graphically depicts the fate of those who had to do battle against man or beast in the amphitheatres of the Roman Empire. Imagine what it must have been like to be one of those unfortunate individuals, pitted against a lion with only a net for protection, or a fully armed soldier with a trident as your only weapon. What chance would you have had?

Ironically, though, in the Christian life we can find ourselves in a similar situation, attacked not physically but spiritually. There is so much that comes into conflict with the way of Christ, both within and outside us. Each day brings a succession of temptations, influences, demands and pressures that threaten to undermine our faith. Little wonder, then, that the Apostle Paul, in his letter to the Romans, spoke of two selves warring within him. Yet, unlike those early gladiators, we do not need to go into battle defenceless, for, as Paul reminds us again, God has given us the resources we need to defend ourselves. Do we make time for prayer and the reading of God's word? Do we look for ways to share the gospel? Do we walk in faith and seek after truth? It is not enough to stroll casually through life trusting that God will protect us. *We* have a part to play, and we neglect it at our peril.

Prayer

Living God,
    teach me never to underestimate the forces
    that conspire against my faith,
    but also never to underestimate the resources
    you have given me to help withstand them.
Teach me to put you at the centre of my life,
    so that I may be equipped for battle
    and ready to defend myself against whatever I may face,
    through the grace of Christ my Lord.
Amen.

Philippians 2:1-11
True humility

If there is any comfort in Christ, any consolation of love, any fellowship of the Spirit, any pity or compassion, complete my joy by having the same love, being one in mind and soul, doing nothing out of personal ambition but, in humility, counting others better than yourselves and being concerned more about their well-being than your own. Let your attitude be the same as that which distinguished Christ Jesus, who, though he was in the form of God, did not regard equality with God as something to be exploited. Instead, he emptied himself, taking the form of a servant and sharing our humanity, and, having taken on human form, he humbled himself to total obedience, even to the point of death – death on a cross. For that reason, God highly exalted him, giving him the name that is above every name, so that at the name of Jesus every being in heaven, on earth and under the earth should kneel, and every tongue should acknowledge that Jesus Christ is Lord, to the glory of God the Father.

Reflection

The mention of humility automatically calls to mind the 'so very 'umble' Uriah Heep of Charles Dickens fame. That fictional character has probably done more to devalue the word 'humble' in popular understanding than anyone else, many subconsciously associating it with a smug, sanctimonious piety. There are, sadly, Christians who reinforce that image, convinced that they should be timid, submissive and diffident, but I do not believe Paul had those characteristics in mind when he wrote to the

Philippians. The words he might have chosen, had he been asked to enlarge on his meaning, would, I think, have been 'modest', 'unassuming', 'unpretentious', 'gentle' – the sort of attributes we see displayed so often and so wonderfully throughout the ministry of Jesus. We see such humility in his birth in a stable, his mixing with social outcasts, his response to the sick and untouchable, his welcoming of little children, his washing of the disciples' feet, his quiet agony on the cross and, finally, in his forgiving, renewing word of peace as the risen Saviour. The Son of God and Lord of all, yet the one who has time for all, however high or low they may be. We cannot hope to emulate him fully, but we should strive nonetheless to show similar humility ourselves: putting self second and others first.

Prayer

Lord Jesus Christ,
    teach me to recognise the topsy-turvy values
    of your kingdom;
    to understand that I am most fully me
    when I lose sight of self,
    that I serve you when I respond to others,
    that I am lifted high when I am brought low;
    and may that realisation shape the kind of person I am
    and the life I live,
    to the glory of your name.
Amen.

Philippians 3:10-14
A journey of discovery

I want to know Christ and the power of his resurrection
and what it means to participate in his sufferings through
identifying with him in his death, if, through that, I may
somehow attain to the resurrection from the dead. Not
that I have already achieved this or reached such a goal,
but I endeavour continually to make it my own, just as
Christ Jesus has made me his own. Friends, I do not
claim to have succeeded; but what I do claim is this:
forgetting what is past and straining forward to what is
yet in store, I strive to reach the goal of the prize of God's
heavenly call in Christ Jesus.

Reflection

I was in a computer shop the other day, waiting to be
served. It proved a long wait, for the customer in front of
me was buying her first computer and understandably
wanted to know what it was she was buying. She didn't
just want any old machine but one that included the very
latest features. Nothing remarkable in that, you might
think, except that the lady in question was in her late
eighties! Outwardly she was alarmingly frail but her
mind was clearly still young, open to explore new tech-
nology, learn more, respond to a new challenge.

We need similar qualities when it comes to the journey
of discipleship, for instead of reaching maturity as Christians we can so easily simply grow old, no longer open to
the renewing power of Christ or the life-giving breath of
his Spirit. Instead of exploring new horizons, we become
stuck in a rut; instead of moving forward, we stand still;

instead of growing, our faith starts to shrink. As Christians we never reach a point where we can claim to have arrived; imagine otherwise and beyond doubt we have lost our way. Living discipleship means recognising that, in this life, we are always on a journey rather than reaching a destination. Whatever we have learned, there is still more to discover. However far we have come, there is still further to go. Lose sight of that and we will have lost sight of what it means to follow Christ.

Prayer

Loving God,
　　travel with me on this journey of faith,
　　your word guiding my footsteps,
　　your power equipping me for service,
　　and your grace each day bringing new beginnings.
Lead me forward,
　　always open to the horizons you have yet to unfold,
　　through Jesus Christ my Lord.
Amen.

Philippians 4:4-7, 10-12
True contentment

Rejoice in the Lord always; I repeat, rejoice! Let your serenity of mind be plain to all. The Lord is near, so do not brood over anything, but in every circumstance, acquaint God with your needs through thankful prayers of supplication, and the peace of God that exceeds all human comprehension will encircle your hearts and minds in Christ Jesus. I exult greatly in the Lord that, after all this time, your concern for me has been re-kindled; indeed, I realise now that you were concerned all along, but were denied the opportunity to show it. Not that I considered myself to be in need, for I have learned to be content whatever the circumstances I am facing. I know what it is to be brought low, and what it is to have my cup overflowing. In all situations, I have learned the secret of being well filled and of going hungry, of having much and having little.

Reflection

Do you pay any attention to advertisements? You may like to think not, but any self-respecting marketing consultant will tell you otherwise. All of us have our weak spots, finding certain things hard to resist, and so, day after day, we are bombarded with advertisements suggesting that the key to happiness is to invest in a new car, computer, dishwasher, holiday abroad and so forth, each subtly portrayed as the one extra we really need. However baseless we may know such claims to be, subliminally we find it hard to resist the siren voices.

Contrast that with the words of the Apostle Paul to the Philippians: 'I have learned to be content whatever the circumstances,' he wrote. It's an astonishing claim, made all the more astonishing by the fact that Paul made it from a prison cell, having repeatedly endured hostility, suffering and persecution on account of his faith. Yet despite innumerable trials he could still speak of possessing everything, for in Christ he had discovered true purpose, inner peace, lasting joy and enduring hope.

What of us? Have we learned to be content in all circumstances? More to the point, have we learned to be content in *any* circumstances? Think about it: that extra possession you acquire – does it really bring happiness or is it simply another insurance risk? Those new clothes – do you really need them or will they merely add to the clutter in your home? That new pursuit you take up – will it fill the aching void within or prove just one more five-minute wonder soon to be abandoned? Paul points us in a different direction, towards what really matters. The riches of this world may satisfy for a moment, but the treasure God offers endures for a lifetime . . . and beyond.

Prayer

Loving God,
    help me to recognise that though serving Christ may
    involve sacrifice and self-denial,
    it also brings lasting fulfilment,
    an inner contentment such as this world
    can never bring.
Teach me that you are able to satisfy my deepest needs,
    granting riches that never tarnish,
    life in all its fullness,
    through Jesus Christ my Lord.
Amen.

Hebrews 12:1-2
Running the race

So, then, since we are surrounded by so great a crowd of witnesses, let us discard everything that encumbers us and the sin that clings so closely, and let us run with perseverance the race set before us, looking to Jesus, the beginning and end of our faith, who, focusing on the joy set before him, endured the cross, disregarding its shame, and has taken his seat at the right hand of the throne of God.

Reflection

When I was a student at Bristol Baptist College, the students of the local Methodist College challenged us to a cross-country run. The day dawned grey and drizzly but I was young, fit and raring to go. As I jogged comfortably along, I held secret hopes of dashing triumphantly over the finishing line in first place. Then we reached it: a steep climb fully half a mile long. I swear to this day that it was the Methodists' secret weapon, carefully chosen as part of the route. It may even be that they had prayed for rain! Whatever the case, the slope was so slippery that, after a couple of steps, my feet gave way and I slid wretchedly back down the hill to where I had started. Before long I was joined by a succession of fellow-Baptists in similar plight. Strangely, the Methodists had no such problem; they sailed up that bank as though they had sprouted wings. Did I ever conquer it? Eventually, yes, but only after several of my colleagues had inspired me through their heroic efforts, scrambling wearily to the top and urging me to give it one last go.

The Christian life can be equally demanding some-times. We start off thinking it's plain sailing but suddenly unexpected obstacles appear in our path. At times we can feel like giving up, but we have the example of those who have gone before us to inspire us onwards, and a respon-sibility to future generations to lead the way in turn. Whether the race is easy or hard, we need to persevere, looking to Jesus and the joy set before us. For me, that day, the incentive was very simple – a hot shower and a cup of tea! The joy we look to through him is something far more wonderful – too wonderful for words.

Prayer

Sovereign God,
    inspire me by the example of Christ
    and the great company of those
    who have gone before me,
    to persevere and run the race,
    faithful to the last,
    in the knowledge that you are waiting to receive me,
    to grant me the joy of your kingdom,
    and the prize of everlasting life,
    through Jesus Christ my Lord.
  Amen.

1 John 4:7-10, 16b
The God of love

Dear friends, let us love one another, because love comes from God; all those who love are born of God and know God. Whoever does not love knows nothing of God, for God is love. God demonstrated his love like this – he sent his only Son into the world in order that we might live through him. In this is love, not that we loved God but that he loved us and sent his Son to be the expiation for our sins. God is love, and all who dwell in love dwell in God, and God dwells in them.

Reflection

On my shelves at home I have a variety of dictionaries and thesauri that, in the course of my editing and writing work, I have had cause to consult on innumerable occasions, and one of the things that invariably surprises me is the sheer complexity of words. A single term can have a wide range of nuances, and many have several completely different meanings. Even everyday terms can prove surprisingly difficult to define. You would have thought, then, that one word in particular would be harder to define than any – the word 'God' – and in a sense that is true, for you could probably find as many understandings of God as there are people. Some would stress his holiness, others his power, others, again, his ineffability, and so I could go on – innumerable aspects of God could justifiably be highlighted.

Yet, in our reading today, we see another approach that, in the light of all of the above, is truly remarkable, for, according to John, one word says it all: God is *love*!

For some, such a definition is far too loose; so vague and insipid that it ends up saying nothing. Yet, the fact is that, when it comes to God, no other word will do, for God *is* love! It's as simple and straightforward as that, this being the one description that says it all, and if we lose that one simple truth, we lose everything. He longs to bless not punish, to give rather than take away; his nature always to have mercy, show kindness and fill our lives with good things. No, we don't deserve such goodness, for we continue to fail him, day after day, but that's what makes God's love so special, for, despite the feebleness of our response, it goes on cleansing, renewing, restoring, forgiving – refusing to let go, come what may. One word to describe the one true God, but what a word and what a God!

Prayer

Living God,
    may your love flow *to* me,
    reaching *down* to bless
    and within to bring joy.
May your love flow through me,
    reaching upwards in worship and outwards in service.
May *your* love kindle *my* love,
    to the glory of your name.
Amen.

Revelation 3:20

Standing at the door

Look, I stand at the door and knock. I will go in and eat with those who hear my voice and open the door, and they will eat with me.

Reflection

I like to think that the pastoral visits I made during my time in the ministry were generally welcomed, but on one occasion at least, my presence was definitely superfluous to requirements. I was calling to see someone who, though a church member, had drifted to the fringe of church life, and whose husband was ambivalent, if not hostile, to all things Christian. My ring at the doorbell met with no response, so I popped a calling card through the letterbox and made my way back down the garden path. For some reason, though, I happened to glance back, and there, looking furtively out the window was the husband in question, checking to make sure the coast was clear. For a second our eyes met. Then, with an expression of utter dismay, the unfortunate fellow dived in desperation behind the settee, determined to avoid me at all costs. Realising I was not wanted I turned and walked nonchalantly away, pretending I'd spotted nothing untoward.

What reaction, I wonder, does Jesus receive when he stands at the door of our lives? Do we fling the door open and welcome him in, or is our response more guarded? Do we open it a little way but keep the security latch fixed, in case he asks more of us than we want to give? Do we open the door briefly, only to usher him out again when commitment doesn't suit us? Do we even keep it firmly closed, pretending we're not in when we'd rather not be disturbed? It's our choice. Jesus will never force his presence upon us, but equally he will never give up knocking in the hope that the door might be opened. More patient than any saint, more persistent than any salesman, more ardent than any suitor, he will always be there seeking entry, so that he can share our life and, more important, so that *we* can share *his*. Is it time you let him?

Prayer

Lord Jesus Christ,
    when you knock at the door and I fail to let you in,
    knock harder,
    until I open.
Amen.